LIFE SCIENCE IN DEPTH

GREEN PLANTS

Sally Morgan

www.heinemann.co.uk/library
Visit our website to find out more information about Heinemann Library books.

To order:
 Phone 44 (0) 1865 888066
 Send a fax to 44 (0) 1865 314091
 Visit the Heinemann bookshop at www.heinemann.co.uk/library to browse
our catalogue and order online.

First published in Great Britain by
Heinemann Library, Halley Court, Jordan Hill,
Oxford OX2 8EJ, part of Harcourt Education.

Heinemann is a registered trademark of
Harcourt Education Ltd.

Editorial: Sarah Shannon and Dave Harris
Design: Richard Parker and Q2A Solutions
Illustrations: Q2A Solutions
Picture Research: Natalie Gray
Production: Chloe Bloom

Originated by Modern Age Repro
Printed and bound in China by South China
Printing Company

10 digit ISBN: 0 431 10910 9
13 digit ISBN: 978 0 431 10910 7

10 09 08 07 06
10 9 8 7 6 5 4 3 2 1

British Library Cataloguing in Publication Data
Morgan, Sally
Green plants.
- (Life science in depth)
571.2
A full catalogue record for this book is available
from the British Library.

Acknowledgements
The publishers would like to thank the following
for permission to reproduce photographs:
Alamy pp. **43** (Bernard Castelein), **44** (David
Sanger), **54** (J.Moers/f1online), **35** (Robert
Harding World Imagery), **56** (Sue Cunningham),
51; Corbis pp. **18** (BSPI), **16** (Bettmann), **31**
(Joseph Sohm), **59**; Getty Images pp. **13**, **21**
(PhotoDisc); Harcourt Education Ltd pp. **23a**,
23b; Oxford Scientific pp. **5**, **37**; Panos
Pictures p. **53** (Caroline Penn); Science Photo
Library pp. **36** (Dr Jeremy Burgess), **1**, **48**
(Francoise Sauze), **39** (Gregory Scott), **47**
(Pascal Goetgheluck), **28** (Steve Gschmeissner).

Cover photograph of plant leaves, reproduced
with permission of Corbis/Bill Ross.

Our thanks to Emma Leatherbarrow for her
assistance in the preparation of this book.

Every effort has been made to contact copyright
holders of any material reproduced in this book.
Any omissions will be rectified in subsequent
printings if notice is given to the publishers.
The paper used to print this book comes from
sustainable resources.

Contents

Words printed in the text in bold, **like this**, are explained in the Glossary.

What are green plants?

Plants are found almost everywhere, from tropical rainforests near the Equator to the Arctic **tundra**, clinging to mountainsides and growing in the oceans. They grow in our gardens and parks and make the countryside green. But they do not just look attractive – they are essential to our very survival. Without plants, animals and people would not be able to survive.

HARNESSING THE SUN

Green plants harness the energy of the Sun and convert it into food, which the plant uses for growth and **reproduction**. This amazing process is called **photosynthesis**, which means making food by using light. It is possible because plants contain a green pigment called **chlorophyll**, which is why they are called green plants. However, not all plants contain chlorophyll. There are a few **parasitic** plants that take their food from other plants rather than make it themselves. Not only do green plants make food but they also make oxygen as a by-product of photosynthesis. Most living organisms need oxygen to breathe. But without plants, there would be almost no oxygen and the Earth's atmosphere would not be breathable.

FOOD CHAINS

Green plants are able to make their own food, but animals cannot. They have to eat a ready-made source of food and one of the most readily available sources of food are plants. Plants are the **producers** of the world's habitats. They are eaten by many different types of herbivores (plant eaters) such as wildebeest and zebra on the African **savannah**, insects in the rainforest, and slugs in the garden.

Herbivores, in turn, are eaten by carnivores (meat-eating animals), such as lions, snakes, and thrushes. Plants are important because they are the start of nearly all **food chains**. Without plants, animals would not be able to survive.

FOOD AND RESOURCES

(Plants are the main source of food for people.) Around the world, millions of hectares of land are used to grow crops such as wheat, rice, maize, and potatoes, as well as many other types of vegetables and fruits. Millions of people rely on wood as their main source of energy to heat their homes and to cook with. Plants supply us with rubber, paper, oil, cotton, and many other fibres. Plants are a valuable source of medicines, too. More than one-third of the world's medicines come from plants.

In this book you will learn about the structure of plants, how they photosynthesize, how they transport water and food, how they reproduce, and why they are so important to people.

There are more than 380,000 different species of plant, and more are being discovered all the time. Tropical rainforests are the most diverse of all the world's habitats with large trees and many smaller plants such as mosses, ferns, and orchids.

Leaves, stems, and roots

A typical plant is made up of leaves, stems, and roots.
The building blocks of each of these are the cells.

THE PLANT CELL

All plant cells are surrounded by a cell membrane and a
cell wall. The cell membrane encloses the **cytoplasm** and a
nucleus. One of the most obvious features is a large **vacuole** –
a fluid-filled structure that usually lies in the middle of the cell.
Some plant cells have **chloroplasts** for photosynthesis.

Most plant cells have a regular
shape with a large vacuole filling
much of the cytoplasm.

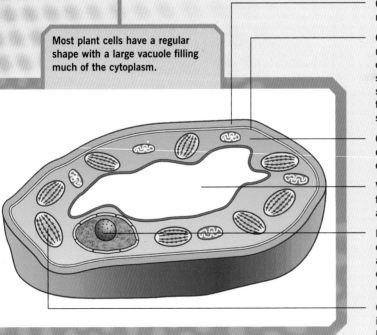

Cell wall – the cell wall is
made up of cellulose.

Cell membrane – the cell
membrane surrounds the
cytoplasm. It has tiny pores
so only small molecules,
such as water, can pass
through. Large molecules,
such as proteins, cannot.

Cytoplasm – the cytoplasm
contains tiny structures
called organelles.

Vacuole – the vacuole is
filled with a watery solution
and gives support to the cell.

Nucleus – the nucleus
controls most of the
activities of the cell,
especially the manufacture
of proteins.

Chloroplast – the chloroplast
is where photosynthesis
happens.

CELLULOSE CELL WALL

The cell wall forms the tough outer surface of the cell. It is made from layers of **cellulose**, and is very strong and slightly elastic. The cell wall protects the cell and holds it in shape. The layers of cellulose are **permeable**. This means there are tiny gaps in the layers which allow substances such as water and oxygen to pass through.

Most living plant cells are **turgid**. This means that they are swollen with water. Water moves into the cell and causes the cytoplasm and vacuole to expand and they push against the wall. The pressure keeps the cell, and the plant, stiff or rigid.

VACUOLES

Plant cells usually have a large central vacuole containing sap. The sap contains sugar and salts, as well as storing food and water. It also helps to keep the cell turgid. The vacuole is small in a newly-formed cell, but as the cell grows, the vacuole gets larger and helps to add bulk to the plant.

CHLOROPLASTS

The chloroplast is where photosynthesis happens. It is packed with green pigment, called chlorophyll. There are chloroplasts in most cells that are exposed to light, often in large numbers. For example, a palisade mesophyll cell in the upper layers of the leaf may have 30 or 40 chloroplasts in its cytoplasm. The chloroplasts can move about within the cell in order to catch the maximum amount of light. Each chloroplast is filled with millions of chlorophyll **molecules**.

Did you know..?

Chloroplasts are extremely small. About 10,000 of them would fit onto the full stop at the end of this sentence.

THE LEAVES

The leaf is a vital organ of a plant. It is made up of a number of different tissues, each of which has a particular role to carry out.

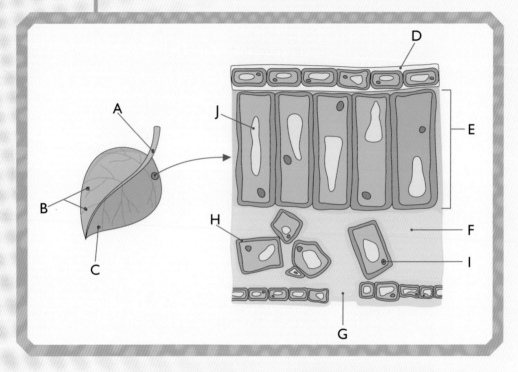

A Midrib – the main vein which brings water to the leaf and takes away the food when it is made

B Network of small veins

C Wide, flat, thin leaf to make photosynthesis as efficient as possible

D Waxy layer – helps to stop water loss from the leaf

E Palisade cells – found at the top of the leaf and packed full of chloroplasts (which contain the green chlorophyll) ready for photosynthesis

F Air spaces – let carbon dioxide move into the cells and oxygen move out

G Stomata – allow gases to move in and out of the leaf

H Cell wall – gives the plant cell strength

I Nucleus – contains all the information to make a new cell and controls the way the cell works

J Vacuole – space in the centre of the plant cell

EVERGREEN

Leaves have **evolved** over millions of years to suit many different **climates**. Evergreen plants keep their leaves all year round. Their leaves are often shiny because they are covered by a thick waxy layer called the cuticle, which helps to reduce water loss. Evergreen plants are found in many different climates. These range from tropical climates where it is important that the plants do not lose water in the dry season, to cold climates where plants need to save water during very cold weather.

Conifers (cone-bearing trees), such as pine and spruce trees, grow in some of the colder regions of the world like Northern Canada and Scandinavia. Their evergreen leaves are tough and needle-shaped. This reduces the surface from which water can evaporate, meaning that the trees do not lose as much water in winter. This is important because the trees are unable to replace water lost from their leaves because the ground is frozen for long periods of time.

DECIDUOUS

Deciduous plants, such as beech and oak trees, drop all their leaves once a year and then grow new ones. Their leaves tend to be broad and flat with a large surface area and therefore lose water easily. Deciduous plants are generally found in **temperate** regions, which have warm summers and cold winters.

In autumn, the leaves go through a series of colour changes from green to orange and red. During this time the plant removes all the valuable **nutrients** from its leaves, causing the leaves to die and fall off. The plants cannot make any food so they "shut down" and become **dormant** until spring.

Deciduous plants would not survive the winter if they kept their leaves. The large leaves would lose too much water and could be damaged by ice and snow. In the spring, a new set of leaves sprout and the tree can photosynthesize again. For the same reasons, deciduous trees are found in places that have dry and wet seasons. Trees lose their leaves at the start of the dry season, again to conserve water.

STEMS

The stem of a plant is designed to support the leaves. Much of this support comes from structures called **vascular bundles**. Some of the cells that form the vascular bundle have extra-strong walls. The vascular bundles grow in a ring to strengthen the stem and stop it from snapping in the wind. Some plants, such as trees, develop woody stems. To do this, the supporting tissues are strengthened with a substance called lignin. Lignin allows these plants to grow much taller than other plants that lack woody stems. These woody stems are covered with a layer of bark.

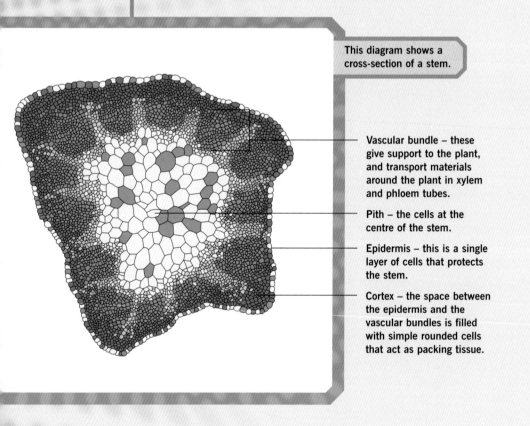

This diagram shows a cross-section of a stem.

Vascular bundle – these give support to the plant, and transport materials around the plant in xylem and phloem tubes.

Pith – the cells at the centre of the stem.

Epidermis – this is a single layer of cells that protects the stem.

Cortex – the space between the epidermis and the vascular bundles is filled with simple rounded cells that act as packing tissue.

ROOTS

The roots of a plant have two main functions. They anchor the plant in the soil and also take up water and dissolved minerals. Roots gain stability from vascular bundles in their centre. Water is easily taken up by the elongated root hair cells (see page 24).

There are two main types of root system – tap root and fibrous roots. As the name suggests, a tap root is made up of one main root that "taps" into the ground. It grows straight down and has smaller roots, called lateral roots, branching off it. In a fibrous root system, there is no one dominant root. Instead, the root system looks like a mass of fibres matted together. Tap roots usually go deeper into the ground than fibrous roots.

Many roots are also used by the plant to store food. For example, a carrot or parsnip is actually the root of a plant that has been packed with **starch** for storage.

There are also some really unusual roots. Epiphytes are plants that grow on other larger plants. Their roots dangle in the air to absorb water, as the plant cannot get water from the ground. Bromeliads are a type of epiphyte that grow on rainforest trees.

STRANGLER FIGS

Strangler figs are found in tropical rainforests. They get their name from the fact that they kill the tree on which they grow.

The fig seeds are spread around the forest by birds that drop them on tree braches. The fig starts to grow on the branch, and sends out many thin roots that grow down the trunk of the tree towards the ground. When the roots reach the ground they grow into the soil and take up water and nutrients. The fig sends out a network of roots that encircle the tree and fuse together. As the roots grow thicker, they squeeze the trunk of the tree and cut off the flow of water and nutrients to its leaves. Eventually the tree dies.

PLANT CLASSIFICATION

There are thousands of different plants and they are divided into different groups. The way that plants are grouped is called classification. All plants belong to the **kingdom** *Plantae*, otherwise known as Plants.

Plants can be divided into three large groups depending on their structure and whether they reproduce by producing **spores** or seeds. The first group is the non-vascular plants, which lack any vascular bundles and produce spores. The second group is seedless vascular plants, which do have vascular bundles but produce spores rather than seeds. The third group is the vascular plants, which have vascular bundles and produce seeds.

NON-VASCULAR PLANTS

Non-vascular plants are also called Bryophytes. They are simple plants with no vascular tissues or woody parts. They have simple leaves with no cuticle. They are restricted to living in damp places because they easily dry out. They do not have flowers. Instead they grow special structures that release spores. There are approximately 20,000 species of non-vascular plants worldwide, including mosses and liverworts.

SCIENCE PIONEERS John Ray

John Ray is often referred to as the father of natural history in the UK. He published many books on plants and animals. In 1682, he published a book on plant classification called *Methodus Plantarum Nova*. In this he set out a natural system of classifying plants based on their form. He studied the shape and structure of the leaves, roots, flowers, and fruits. His system was the first to divide flowering plants into **monocotyledons** and **dicotyledons**. This formed the basis of modern day methods of classifying plants.

SEEDLESS VASCULAR PLANTS

There are more than 7,000 species of seedless vascular plants including ferns, horsetails, and club mosses. They have vascular tissues so can grow to a larger size than the Bryophytes. These plants do not produce flowers and seeds. Instead they produce spores. The leaves, known as fronds, vary widely in size and shape. They are called fronds because the spore-producing structures are found on their under surface.

These ferns are seedless vascular plants – you can see the pattern of fronds that uncurl as they grow.

SEED-PRODUCING PLANTS

Conifers, cycads, and flowering plants all produce seeds. Conifers are large plants with woody trunks (see page 10). Most have evergreen leaves and their seeds grow inside protective cones. Cycads are plants that look a bit like small palms but they produce cones. Flowering plants, also called angiosperms, are the main plant group on Earth. There are more than 250,000 different species.

Photosynthesis

Plants are not the only organisms that can use sunlight to make food, but they are the most successful. About 99 percent of the sunlight that reaches the Earth is absorbed by the land and the oceans or reflected back into space. Just one percent is absorbed by plant leaves and used to make food.

Green plants use light, carbon dioxide, and water to make, or synthesize, food such as sugars and starch in a process called photosynthesis. This process is explained by the following equation:

$$\text{CARBON DIOXIDE} + \text{WATER} \xrightarrow{\text{LIGHT}} \text{SUGAR} + \text{OXYGEN}$$

This equation makes photosynthesis look quite simple, but in fact it is a very complicated process, involving many reactions. Two raw materials are needed for photosynthesis – water and carbon dioxide. Water is carried up the stem from the roots to the leaf and carbon dioxide enters the leaf from the air. The other important part is the chlorophyll. When sunlight strikes the chlorophyll molecules in the chloroplast, the light energy is converted into chemical energy. This chemical energy is used to make sugars and starch from water and carbon dioxide. Oxygen is also produced and this moves out of the leaf.

PHOTOSYNTHETIC PIGMENTS

The reason that plants can trap light energy and use it to make food is because they contain chlorophyll. Chlorophyll is found in the chloroplasts of palisade mesophyll cells, spongy mesophyll cells, and the guard cells. Chlorophyll is a large molecule and it can absorb certain wavelengths of light, in particular red and blue light. The green light is reflected, and this is why plants look green.

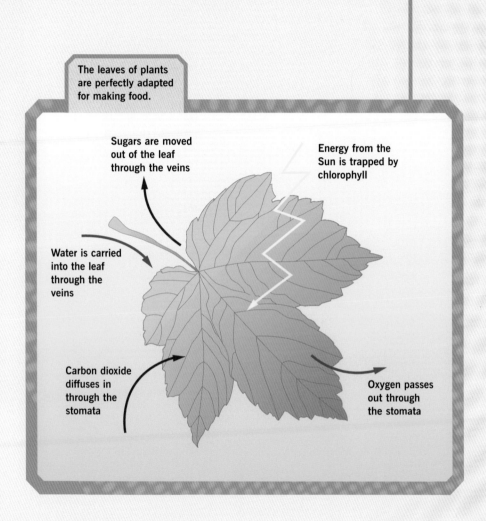

The leaves of plants are perfectly adapted for making food.

Sugars are moved out of the leaf through the veins

Energy from the Sun is trapped by chlorophyll

Water is carried into the leaf through the veins

Carbon dioxide diffuses in through the stomata

Oxygen passes out through the stomata

Did you know..?

Organisms that can make their own food are called autotrophs, which literally means "self-feeding". Most autotrophs are plants. There are also some **micro-organisms** that use light, like plants, to produce food, and others that use chemicals as their energy source.

SUGAR AND STARCH

The main product of photosynthesis is sugar. Sugar cannot be stored in the cell, so it either has to be made into something that can be stored or moved to another part of the plant. Usually, the cell quickly converts the sugar to starch, which is stored as grains in the chloroplast. Some of the sugar is used to make other compounds such as fats and **amino acids**, the building blocks of proteins. Some of the sugar is moved in the phloem (the tissue in the stem that transports sugar) to the places that are growing fast, for example new leaves and shoot tips, where it is used as food.

Much of the sugar is taken to the roots, where it is stored as starch grains in the packing tissues. In some plants, the starch is stored in the roots, and for that reason they make good vegetables, for example carrots and parsnips. Some plants store their starch in **tubers**, for example potatoes. A tuber is a swelling found underground at the end of a stem. During the summer months the potato plant makes lots of tubers, and they survive underground through winter. In spring, the starch in the tubers is broken down into sugar, which can be used to fuel new growth.

SCIENCE PIONEERS Melvin Calvin

Melvin Calvin discovered many of the secrets of photosynthesis and in 1961 he was awarded the Nobel Prize for Chemistry. He worked out how carbon dioxide was used in photosynthesis. This part of the process of photosynthesis was named "The Calvin Cycle" after him.

Melvin Calvin and his team of scientists unravelled the secrets of one of the most important reactions on Earth.

KEY EXPERIMENT starch test on variegated leaves

Starch is one of the products of photosynthesis, so its presence can be used as proof that photosynthesis has taken place. A variegated leaf (see page 19) is used in this experiment as it has green areas that can carry out photosynthesis and yellow areas that cannot. First, the leaf is boiled in water for about 30 seconds to break the cell walls. Then, it is transferred to a tube containing 95 percent alcohol, which is placed in a hot-water bath. The alcohol is allowed to boil, and this removes the pigment from the leaf. The leaf is removed and rinsed in water, then placed on a tile. Iodine is poured over the leaf. Iodine is a chemical that can test for the presence of starch – it is normally yellow in colour, but it turns a dark blue-black colour when starch is present. With a variegated leaf, only the green areas of the leaf give a positive result for starch.

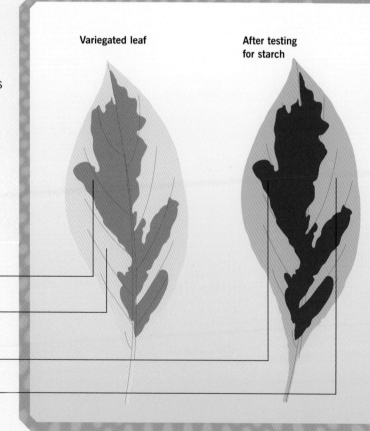

Variegated leaf

After testing for starch

Green colour indicates chlorophyll in cells

Yellow/white area indicates that no chlorophyll is in the cell

Dark blue-black colour indicates starch is present

Yellow-brown colour indicates no starch present

LEAF DESIGN

Plant leaves are specially **adapted** for their role of photosynthesis. This means that their shape and structure are the best design for carrying out their job. Most leaves tend to have a large surface area so that they can trap as much light as possible. Leaves are usually thin so that gases, such as carbon dioxide and oxygen, do not have to travel very far. The upper epidermis is often protected by a cuticle, which helps to reduce water loss. The lower epidermis has stomata, which allow carbon dioxide to get in more quickly and oxygen to escape. The leaf is supported by a network of veins, which are also responsible for moving materials into and out of the leaf.

The leaves of these trees are carefully arranged to form a mosaic so that they do not shade each other and they can absorb the maximum amount of light.

LEAF SHAPE

Leaves vary in shape. Often, this is an adaptation to where they grow. In a forest, the tall trees form what is called the canopy and lower growing shrubs form the understorey. The tall trees receive a lot of light, so their leaves tend to be smaller in size, for example the beech or the oak. The plants in the understorey are shaded and their leaves tend to be larger so they have a greater surface area for absorbing light.

There are three leaf-type shapes: a simple leaf, a pinnate-compound leaf, and a palmate leaf.

simple

palmate

pinnate

SIMPLE AND COMPOUND

Leaves can be simple or compound. A simple leaf has only one part that attaches to the branch, but it can have many different shapes. Beech and oak trees have simple leaves. Compound leaves have many parts, called leaflets. In pinnate-compound leaves, the leaflets are arranged in pairs along the leaf stem. Ash trees and roses have pinnate-compound leaves. Other plants have leaves in which the leaflets are spread out like fingers on the palm of your hand. These are called palmate leaves. For example, the horse-chestnut leaf has five or seven leaflets with jagged edges, and the leaflets are joined at the base of the leaf.

COLOURED LEAVES

Not all leaves are green. There are some that are described as variegated, because they have areas that lack any chlorophyll and are white or yellow in colour. Often plants in tropical regions, where the Sun is powerful, have leaves that are tinged with red. Some scientists say that the red pigment protects the chlorophyll from **ultraviolet** damage from sunlight. The pigment is acts a bit like a sunscreen.

THE IMPORTANCE OF OXYGEN

Oxygen is a very important gas. In fact, about 21 percent of the atmosphere is oxygen and this is maintained by green plants. Nearly all organisms, including animals and plants, need oxygen for **respiration**. Respiration is a process that takes place in cells. Foods such as glucose are broken down in the cells, and this releases the chemical energy that is needed by the organism to function. The waste products of respiration are carbon dioxide, water, and heat.

Plants produce oxygen when they photosynthesize. During the day, they produce more oxygen than they use in respiration, so oxygen leaves the plant and enters the atmosphere. This maintains the level of oxygen in the atmosphere. However, plants only photosynthesize in the light, so at night they just respire and use up oxygen.

KEY EXPERIMENT
pondweed and oxygen production

Oxygen is a by-product of photosynthesis, so measuring the amount of oxygen produced by a plant is a good way of working out the rate of photosynthesis. In water plants, such as pondweed, the oxygen comes off as bubbles, which can be trapped. In this experiment, a sprig of pondweed is placed in water and the oxygen given off is collected in a test tube. By measuring the amount of oxygen given off in the bubbles, the rate of photosynthesis can be worked out.

GREENHOUSE GASES

Greenhouse gases are essential for all life on Earth. Without them, the temperature of the Earth would be too cold for life. Greenhouse gases allow sunlight to pass through the atmosphere but they stop heat escaping – a bit like a greenhouse where the glass allows the sunlight to pass through but prevents the heat from escaping. There are a number of different greenhouse gases and carbon dioxide is one of the most important. It is produced by the respiration of organisms such as bacteria, plants, and animals, and from the burning of wood and **fossil fuels** such as coal, oil, and gas.

Scientists are concerned that as large areas of forests, especially rainforests, are being cleared there are fewer plants to take up carbon dioxide. As the concentration of carbon dioxide and other greenhouse gases in the atmosphere increases, more heat is trapped. This is causing the Earth to get slowly warmer. This warming may be only by a degree or two but it is enough to disrupt the world's climate and may cause the ice caps to start to melt and sea levels to rise.

It is estimated that 31 million hectares of tropical rainforest are cut down every year. That is an area about the size of Poland. The loss of these trees means that less carbon dioxide is being used in photosynthesis and less oxygen is being produced.

ESSENTIAL MINERALS

Plants cannot survive on just carbon dioxide and water; they also need **minerals** (nutrients) from the soil. These minerals are used to make proteins and many other substances needed by the plant for healthy growth. The three most important minerals are nitrogen (N) in the form of nitrates, phosphorus (P) as phosphate, and potassium (K). Plants also need trace quantities of other minerals such as magnesium, calcium, iron, and sulphur. If the plant is deficient in any of these essential minerals, it will show signs of poor growth.

Mineral	Role	Deficiency effects
Nitrogen	Used in amino acids and proteins	Poor growth, yellow leaves
Phosphorus	Used in proteins, especially enzymes and energy-rich molecules	Poor growth, dull green leaves with brown edges
Potassium	Used in proteins, including enzymes	Yellow-edged leaves, plants die early
Calcium	Needed for cell walls	Poor buds, stunted growth
Iron	Needed to make chlorophyll	Yellow leaves
Magnesium	Used in chlorophyll	Yellow leaves
Sulphur	Used in proteins	Yellow leaves, poor growth

FERTILIZERS

Farmers need to make sure their crops get enough of the essential nutrients, especially nitrogen, phosphorus, and potassium. They do this by adding **fertilizers**. One natural source of fertilizer is farmyard manure. It contains straw mixed with the dung and urine of farm animals such as cattle. This good source of minerals is spread over the ground where it rots down. As it decays, it slowly releases its nutrients back into the soil where they can be used by the crops.

Farmers may choose to use artificial fertilizers, which are manufactured in factories from chemicals. Materials such as bone, horn, and fishmeal are also used in artificial fertilizers. They can be spread easily over the land and, because they are **soluble**, they are carried into the soil by rain. Artificial fertilizers get minerals to the plant roots quickly, but they can also be washed away more easily.

SCIENCE PIONEERS Wilhelm Knop

One of the first people to realize that plants needed nutrients such as nitrogen and potassium was the German scientist Wilhelm Knop. In 1865, he made up a solution that he considered to be ideal for plant growth as it contained all of the nutrients required by a plant. All he had to do was suspend the roots of a young seedling in the solution and it would grow. He showed that each nutrient was essential for growth by repeating the experiment many times. Each time he left out just one of the nutrients, and the plant did not grow properly.

The effect of removing one of the essential nutrients for plant growth is shown clearly here.

Moving water around

Water is essential to the survival of a plant. Plants have to be able to take up water from the ground and move it through the roots and stem to where it is needed. Water also plays an important role in supporting the plant.

TAKING UP WATER

Plants take up water through their roots. Roots are specially adapted to the role of absorbing water from the soil. The most important feature is the large surface area of roots. The greater the surface area, the greater the amount of water that can be taken up. Tiny hairs found around the root tip greatly increase the surface area of the root. It is these root hairs that are responsible for taking up water. The water enters the root hairs by a process called osmosis.

Osmosis is the movement of water molecules across a cell membrane from where they are in high concentration to where they are in lower concentration. Put simply, osmosis tries to balance the concentrations on either side of a membrane. So, if there is a higher concentration of water on one side than the other, molecules of water will cross the membrane until the concentrations on both sides match, or until the plant cell is full, or turgid, and cannot absorb any more water.

In plant cells, there are tiny gaps in the membrane that water can pass through but larger molecules, such as protein and sugar, cannot. The cytoplasm and vacuole of the root hair cell contains a lot of proteins and sugar molecules and this means they have a lower water concentration than soil water. This means that water moves from the soil, through the membrane, into the root hair cell where there are fewer water molecules. Minerals are also absorbed with the water molecules.

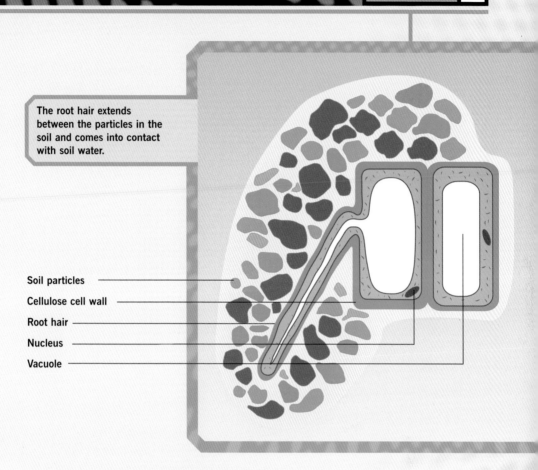

The root hair extends between the particles in the soil and comes into contact with soil water.

Soil particles

Cellulose cell wall

Root hair

Nucleus

Vacuole

THE BALANCING ACT

Plants must keep a balance between the surface area available for making food, the leaves, and the surface area available for taking up water and minerals, the roots. If there are a lot of leaves compared with the roots, the roots may not be able to absorb enough water for the leaves and the leaves will suffer from a lack of water. A young plant tends to have lots of roots and fewer shoots. As the plant gets older, it produces more leaves to help it to grow. When a plant's roots are damaged, during a transplant, for example, many of the smaller roots are left behind. This disturbs the balance and may harm the plant. The plant may lose some or many of its leaves, but it will grow new roots quickly, so it can regain its root-shoot balance.

TRANSPIRATION

Once the water is inside the root, the plant needs to move it up to the leaves where it can be used for photosynthesis. Water passes from the root hair cell across the cortex to the endodermis around the central vascular bundle. The cells of the endodermis play an important role. They control the entry and exit of materials to the central vascular bundle. The water then passes into the xylem vessels and is carried up the stem to the leaves.

Transpiration is the evaporation of water from the surfaces of the leaves. As water evaporates, more water is pulled into the leaf to replace it. This in turn, pulls water up the stem from the root, and creates a continual stream of water from the roots to the leaves.

Transpiration can be affected by many factors. More water evaporates on a warm, sunny day and on a windy day than on a still, rainy day. Most of the water evaporates through the stomata, especially on the lower surface of the leaf, during the day. The stomata play an important role because they provide the main route by which water can escape from the plant into the atmosphere. Less transpiration occurs from the upper epidermis because of the waxy cuticle, which helps to prevent evaporation. In most plants, the stomata are open in the daylight hours because the plant needs carbon dioxide for photosynthesis, and they close at night. Therefore, much less transpiration takes place at night.

Did you know..?

A single mature oak tree can give off around 400 litres (90 gallons) of water per day through transpiration. An acre of corn can give off around 15,000 litres (3,300 gallons) in a day!

KEY EXPERIMENT potometer

A potometer is a device used for measuring the rate of water uptake of a leafy plant shoot. The main reason that water is taken up by a cut shoot is transpiration. By changing the surrounding atmospheric conditions, the effect of wind, heat, and humidity on transpiration can be measured.

A potometer consists of a length of very fine tubing, called a capillary tube, filled with water. It is attached to the cut shoot at one end and a source of water at the other. A bubble is introduced into the capillary tube. As the plant takes up water, the bubble moves. The distance the bubble travels in a given time is determined by the rate of water uptake by the plant.

The potometer measures the uptake of water by a leafy shoot. The air bubble in the capillary tube is timed to see how long it takes to move between two marks on the tube.

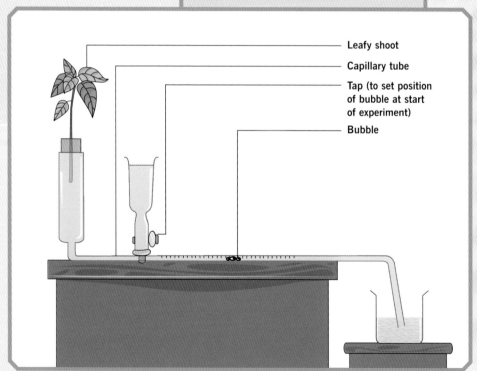

Leafy shoot

Capillary tube

Tap (to set position of bubble at start of experiment)

Bubble

XYLEM TISSUE

Water is moved around the plant by xylem tissue and its cells are specialized for this purpose. The xylem tissue is made up of xylem vessels. These vessels are formed by chains of cells, one on top of another. The cell walls are strengthened by lignin. The presence of lignin causes the cells to die and their end walls break down to form a hollow tube.

The xylem vessels (which you can see in the middle of this stem) are hollow but strong as they are strengthened by lignin. The lignin kills the cells, and they then lose their contents and their end walls to form a strong tube.

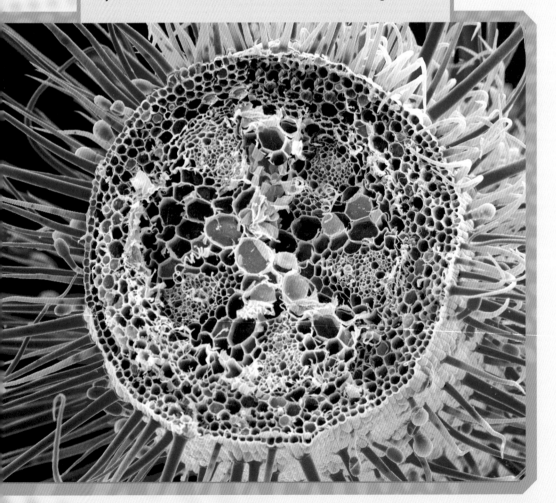

Julius von Sachs

The work of the German **botanist**, Julius von Sachs, in
the second half of the 19th century, helped people to
understand more about how plants function. One of his
major areas of interest was the movement of water in
plants. He discovered that the water taken up by the roots
of a plant moves in xylem vessels. In 1865, he proved that
chlorophyll is not spread evenly throughout the plant but is
located in special structures within plant cells. These were
later called chloroplasts. He found that the green pigment
(chlorophyll) in plants is where glucose is made, and that
the glucose is usually stored as starch. He also studied the
formation of growth rings in trees and the influence of
gravity and sunlight on plant growth.

WATER FOR SUPPORT

Some plants use woody tissue for support, for example the
trunk of a tree. Other plants gain their support from water.
When there is plenty of water, the vacuole in the cell is kept
large and firm and it pushes out on the cell wall, keeping the
shape of the cell. The neighbouring cells push against each
other and this makes the leaf or the stem very stiff. If the plant
cannot get enough water, there is less water in the vacuole
and the cells lose support. This means they do not push
against each other and the plant wilts. A plant can only afford
to lose so much water before it starts to wilt, and if it does not
get a new supply of water quickly, it could end up getting too
dehydrated to survive. Some plants are tolerant of **drought**
and can recover, but many plants die.

LIFE IN THE DESERT

One of the characteristic plants of the North American deserts is the cactus, a plant that has adapted to living in dry habitats. Other plants found in the desert include succulent plants that have fleshy leaves in which they store water. Cacti and succulents can survive on very little water, whereas a plant used to living in a habitat with plenty of water would quickly die. They can recover quickly too – as soon as the rains fall, the roots absorb water and the plant rehydrates its tissues.

CACTI

Cacti are unusual plants as most do not have leaves. Instead their leaves are considerably reduced to form spines. This reduces their surface area, so less water can evaporate. This saves water compared with a large flat leaf. Their stems tend to be fleshy and can expand to store water. They are covered by a thick cuticle, which reduces the evaporation of water. Some cacti are very hairy and this also helps to trap water and prevent it from evaporating. The hairs provide good insulation on cold desert nights. Many cacti have an extensive root system in the ground so that they can absorb every last drop of water.

OTHER ADAPTATIONS TO DESERT LIFE

Some other desert-living plants have adaptations, too. They may not have spines but their leaves are rolled up to reduce the surface area and to trap any moisture inside the leaf. Some plants have a different strategy for surviving in the desert. After the rains, many deserts are covered in a carpet of flowers. These are the short-lived plants, called annuals, which live for just one year before they produce seeds and die. Annuals, such as poppies, survive the dry season as **seeds** in the ground. When the rains come, the seeds **germinate** and within weeks the flowers appear. They produce a lot of seeds and as soon as the ground dries up again, they die.

The prickly pear cactus has thick stems that can expand to hold more water. The stems are covered in spines, which protect the plant from grazing animals.

SALT MARSHES

Plants that live in salt marshes may be surrounded by water but it is salt water. Plants need fresh water, so plants that live in salt marshes have adaptations for storing water just like the desert plants. They have fleshy leaves and thick cuticles and leaves that will roll up.

AQUATIC PLANTS

Plants that actually live in the water have a different set of problems. They are surrounded by water all the time and they have to stop too much water entering their cells. Plants that live in water also need to stay near to the surface in order to get enough light for photosynthesis. Many have large air spaces in their stems and leaves so they can float in the water.

Flowers, fruits, and seeds

Flowers are specialized structures, which are designed for one purpose – reproduction. They produce seeds through sexual reproduction. The flower develops within a bud, which is protected by leaf-like structures called sepals. When the flower opens, the sepals either fold back or drop off.

Flowers can look very different but they all have either **stamen**, which are the male reproductive organs, or **carpels**, the female reproductive organs. The majority of flowers have both stamens and carpels, but there are some that are single sex. A stamen is made up of an anther and a stalk called a filament. Pollen grains develop inside the anthers. A carpel consists of a stigma, a style, and an **ovary**. The egg cell is in the **ovule** that lies inside the ovary.

POLLINATION AND FERTILIZATION

Reproduction in flowering plants involves two processes – **pollination** and **fertilization**. Pollination is the transfer of pollen from the stamens of one flower to the carpel of another. Fertilization occurs when a pollen cell joins up with the egg cell in the carpel. Once the egg cell has been fertilized, the carpels develop into **fruits** and seeds, which are dispersed away from the parent plant. Later, when conditions are suitable, these seeds may germinate and grow into new plants.

The main problem for the plant is how to get the pollen from the anther of one flower to the carpel of another flower. There are two main ways in which this can be done – insect pollination or wind pollination. Insect pollination, as the name suggests, involves insects or other animals, such as birds or bats, carrying the pollen from one flower to another. In wind pollination, the pollen is carried between flowers by the wind.

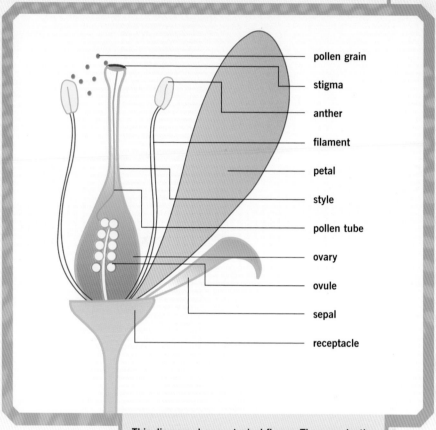

- pollen grain
- stigma
- anther
- filament
- petal
- style
- pollen tube
- ovary
- ovule
- sepal
- receptacle

This diagram shows a typical flower. The reproductive organs of a plant vary widely in appearance between species, which we see in the huge variety of flowers in our gardens and parks.

INSECT POLLINATION

Insect-pollinated flowers first have to attract the insects or other animals that pick up the pollen and carry it to other flowers. This is the purpose of the flower. The petals are usually brightly coloured and very attractive to the insects. Many have special guidelines, which are visible only to insects, and lead the insect directly to the nectar. The flowers "bribe" insects into visiting by providing free food in the form of nectar, which is a sugary liquid loved by insects because it is a good source of energy.

INSECT-POLLINATED FLOWERS

The structure of an insect-pollinated flower varies from species to species. Some have large, relatively simple flowers with separate petals, while others have a more complex structure in which the petals are fused together to form tubes. The buttercup is a relatively simple insect-pollinated flower. Its petals are bright yellow and form a ring around the stamens and carpels. There is plenty of space for the insects to land. The nectar is produced in the nectaries, which are positioned at the base of the petals to encourage the insects to go deep into the flower. There are usually a number of filaments and they stand upright holding up the anthers.

The pollen is sticky and spiky and as the insects walk over the flower, the hairs on their bodies pick up the pollen grains. The top part of the carpel is called the stigma and it is slightly pointed and covered with short, thick hairs. These catch the pollen grains from insect bodies as the insects push past.

Once they are attached to the stigma, the pollen grains send out a long tube called a pollen tube that grows down through the style, and into the ovary and ovule. A male nucleus passes through the pollen tube into the ovule, where it fertilizes the egg cell. This forms a new cell called a zygote, which grows into a new plant. Once fertilization has happened, the flower withers and dies. The ovule develops into a seed while the ovary forms a fruit to protect it.

OTHER POLLINATORS

Insects are not the only animals that pollinate flowers. Snails and slugs may slither over flowers and carry pollen in the trail of thick, sticky fluid that they make as they move. Some birds pollinate flowers. Birds can see colour very well, particularly red. So many red flowers are pollinated by birds. Humming birds, in particular, are attracted to red, orange, and yellow flowers. In the rainforests, the fruit bat is an important pollinator. They fly many kilometres each night in the search for nectar. When they find the flowers, they drink the nectar and at the same time pick up pollen.

Other flowers rely on flies for pollination. The huge *Rafflesia* flower produces a horrible smell like rotting meat and this attracts flies. As they crawl around the flower in search of the meat, they pick up pollen and then carry it to other flowers.

The huge *Rafflesia* flower is the world's largest flower. It is found only in the rainforests of southeast Asia. It is about 1 metre (39 inches) across and can weigh up to 11 kilograms (24 pounds)! The plant is a parasite on the *Tetrastigma* vine and it produces no leaves, stems, or roots. The only part that can be seen is the flower or bud.

WIND-POLLINATED FLOWERS

The other way for flowers to be pollinated is by wind pollination. Wind-pollinated flowers are often small and inconspicuous since they do not need to attract insects. They do not produce nectar and they do not have any scent. Most trees and grasses have wind-pollinated flowers. The anthers are long and thin and they dangle out of the flowers. The anthers are loosely joined to the filaments and they vibrate even in the slightest breeze. They release large quantities of very small, light pollen grains that are easily carried away by the wind. The stigma is long and feathery and it also hangs outside the flower so that it can trap pollen floating past in the air.

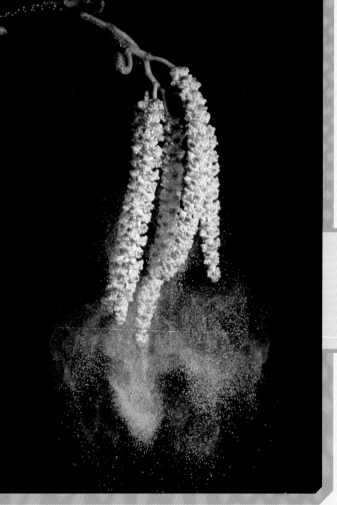

The male flower of the hazel is called a catkin. This is made up of lots of individual flowers joined together. The stamens dangle in the wind and release clouds of pollen. The female flower is a small red structure that has three feathery stigmas to trap pollen.

HAY FEVER

Wind-pollinated flowers need to produce great quantities of pollen to be sure that at least some pollen grains will reach the stigmas of other flowers. In summer, many people suffer from hay fever, which is like having a very bad cold. These people are allergic to the pollen in the air and sneeze a lot when they are outside. On rainy days, the amount of pollen in the air (called the pollen count) is low because rain washes the air clean of dust particles and pollen grains. On sunny, dry days, the pollen count can be very high.

CROSS-POLLINATION

There are two different types of pollination. These are cross-pollination and self-pollination. When pollen is transferred from the anthers of one flower to the stigma of another flower it is called cross-pollination. However, sometimes the pollen from the anther of one flower is transferred to the stigma of the same flower, or a flower on the same plant. This is called self-pollination. Cross-pollination is better than self-pollination. When flowers are cross-pollinated, their seeds germinate and grow into strong, healthy plants. Seeds from self-pollinated flowers tend to produce weaker, less healthy plants. Most flowers are specially adapted to help prevent self-pollination. The stamens and carpels in the same flower mature at different times. For example, in the buttercup the anthers mature first and by the time the carpels are mature, the anthers have died and no longer produce pollen. This ensures that the flowers cannot be self-pollinated and are only cross-pollinated. There are some species of plant that actually produce male-only and female-only plants to make self-pollination impossible.

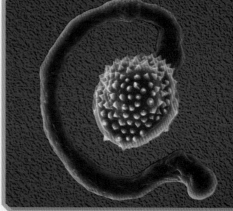

The pollen tubes have to be long in order to reach the egg in the ovary.

FRUITS AND SEEDS

After fertilization, the flower withers and the ovary develops into a fruit. The ovule becomes the seed, which contains the embryonic plant (the part of the seed that develops into a new plant). It is important that the new plant develops away from the parent plant. Otherwise, the young plants would have to compete for light, water, and minerals with the much larger, stronger parent plant. It is much better if the seeds germinate in another area. Since plants cannot move from place to place, they have developed other ways to make certain that their seeds are taken well away from them. This is called seed dispersal. Some plants use animals to disperse their seeds, others use the wind, and a few actually explode.

FLYING AND FLOATING

Some fruits have thin wing-like structures. Instead of falling straight to the ground, their "wings" cause them slowly to spiral their way down to the ground so they land away from the parent plant. Sycamore, ash, and maple trees all produce fruits of this type.

In some fruits, the style and the stigma change into a feathery parachute, which catches the wind. The dandelion clock is made from hundreds of these parachute fruits, each containing a seed. Some plants produce fruits called pods, which contain rows of seeds inside them, for example peas, beans, and lupins. When these fruits dry out, the two sides of the pod suddenly separate, sometimes with great force, so that the seeds are thrown far away from the parent plant.

HITCHING A LIFT

Animals can disperse seeds in different ways. Some fruits, for example the fruits of burdock and goosegrass, are covered by many tiny hooks, which get caught in the fur of an animal as it brushes against the plant. As the animal moves along, the fruit gets more and more tangled up in its fur until it touches the skin of the animal. The animal uses its legs or teeth to pull the fruit out of its fur and drops it on the ground, well away from the parent plant.

Other fruits are fleshy, sweet, and edible, such as grapes, oranges, and berries. Many animals eat these fruits, especially birds. Usually, the animal picks up the fruit and moves away to eat it. It spits out the seed (or seeds) from the centre of the fruit. If the conditions are right, these seeds will germinate where they land. Some birds eat the whole fruit, including the seeds. These seeds pass straight through their digestive system unharmed and are passed out of the bird's body with the rest of the waste. By this time the animal has moved a long way from the parent plant and the seed is dropped onto the ground surrounded by a supply of manure, which acts as fertilizer and helps its early growth.

Birds like this are vitally important to many species of plants.

SEED GERMINATION

Seeds are remarkable structures. They can lie dormant in the soil for many years before germinating. They consist of an **embryo** plant, surrounded by a food store, and protected by a tough seed coat. The food store is used to fuel the early growth of the young seedling until it is able to grow its own leaves and can photosynthesize.

Many environmental factors can affect seed germination. Light intensity, day length, presence of water, gravity, temperature, oxygen availability, seed condition, and age can all affect seed germination. Some seeds with heavy seed coats will only germinate after the seed coat has been damaged.

WHEN TO GERMINATE?

The time of year that a seed germinates is also very important. If they germinate at the wrong time, they may die. For example, sycamore seeds are produced in autumn and they are carried away from the parent plant on the wind. If the seed germinates immediately, the young plant may be killed by the cold winter weather. To overcome this problem, sycamore seeds lie dormant in the soil until the spring. They are triggered to germinate when the soil is moist and the soil temperature is warm.

FIRST GROWTH

In order to germinate, a seed has to absorb water. The water causes the seed to swell and this splits the seed coat. This is also the trigger for a number of **enzymes** to start breaking down food stores and releasing energy that the seedling needs to grow. The root, or radicle, is the first part of the young plant to grow. It grows out through the seed coat and down into the soil. Then the shoot appears and grows in the opposite direction. The seed leaf is called a cotyledon. In some seeds, the cotyledon is swollen with food and stays within the seed. In others, the cotyledon is the first leaf to appear. It is a rounded, fleshy leaf, which looks nothing like the true leaves that appear later.

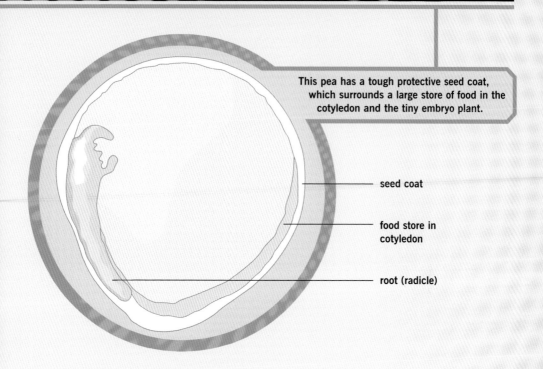

This pea has a tough protective seed coat, which surrounds a large store of food in the cotyledon and the tiny embryo plant.

seed coat

food store in cotyledon

root (radicle)

KEY EXPERIMENT seed germination

Seeds require certain conditions before they can germinate. This prevents them germinating at the wrong time of year. Many tree seeds only germinate after they have experienced freezing temperatures. By germinating seeds in different conditions, it is possible to find out which factors are important. Seeds of the same type can be placed on damp filter paper in Petri dishes and then some placed in the dark and some in the light at the same temperature. At the end of two weeks, the number of seeds that germinate in the light and dark can be counted. It is also possible to investigate the effect of temperature on seed germination.

Plants for food

Plants are an important source of food for many animals and people. Since they produce food by photosynthesis, they are known as producers and they have an important role in the food chain.

FOOD CHAINS

A food chain is a series of food transfers in which one organism feeds on another. Each time an organism is eaten by another, there is a transfer of energy. In most food chains, the initial source of energy is sunlight and this is absorbed by green plants. A simple example of a food chain is:

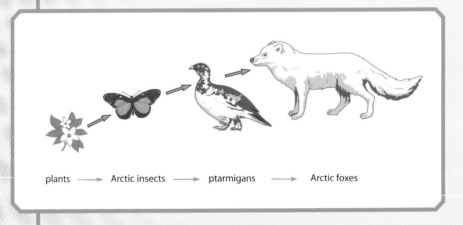

plants ⟶ Arctic insects ⟶ ptarmigans ⟶ Arctic foxes

In this food chain, the plant provides the insects with food. Plants provide animals with a range of foods. Some animals feed on the leaves while others eat just the fruits. Animals such as pigs will dig in the soil to reach the roots that are rich in starch. Insects and hummingbirds feed on nectar.

Animals like this rhino are able to digest plant material. They must eat a lot of plants to get enough food to survive.

DIGESTING CELLULOSE

Cellulose makes up the bulk of a plant but it is a tough material to digest. Animals that eat plant foods need a special enzyme called cellulase to be able to break down the cellulose into sugar. However, mammals cannot produce this enzyme by themselves. Most mammal herbivores have to rely on the secretions of bacteria and other micro-organisms in their gut to break down the cellulose. People cannot digest cellulose either, since we do not have the correct gut micro-organisms. However, cellulose still forms an essential part of a healthy human diet as fibre. Fibre provides bulk, which helps food to move through the gut.

TROPHIC LEVELS, BIOMASS, AND ENERGY

The organisms within a food chain fit into different trophic or feeding levels according to the food they eat. Plants are always in the first trophic level as they are producers. This first trophic level has the greatest number of individuals and contains the greatest **biomass**, that is, the mass of living material. The next level is the primary consumer, then the secondary consumer, and tertiary consumer, and so on. As you go from the first to the higher levels, the number of organisms decreases. For example, there are fewer ladybirds than aphids. This is because ladybirds feed on aphids, so there cannot be more ladybirds than aphids. The biomass of the ladybirds is also lower.

PLANTS AS CROPS

People rely on plants for much of their food. Many plants are described as staple foods because we eat them every day as our main source of energy. Good examples would be cereals and potatoes. These foods are rich in **carbohydrates** and fats. We also rely on a range of fruits and vegetables for the minerals and vitamins we need in our diet.

Many types of plants are grown as crops (cultivated plants). Crop plants have been improved over the years by careful plant breeding so that they produce greater yields or larger seeds.

Rice is the staple food in Asia and Africa. Rice plants are planted in shallow water in fields called paddies. Often the paddies are terraced down a mountainside. As the growing season continues, the paddies dry up and the rice is harvested.

For example, wheat has been developed from a wild grass species. Over hundreds of years farmers have selected plants with bigger and more numerous seeds. Today, a wheat seed is many times larger than that of a grass seed.

CEREALS

Cereals are grass plants such as wheat, barley, maize, or rice. They are wind-pollinated with long blade-like leaves and the seeds are produced in a spike. Cereals produce seeds that contain carbohydrates. The seed can be eaten whole or the seed coat removed. Wheat, for example, is ground to remove the tough outer seed coat, leaving white starch, which can be used as flour.

Wheat is grown in temperate areas around the world, where there are cold winters but warm, wet summers, and a fertile soil, for example North America, Europe, Russia, and Australia. Maize requires a warmer climate than wheat, so is grown in the more southerly North American States, South America, Africa, and parts of Asia and Australia. In India and southeast Asia, the climate and soil are more suited to growing rice, which requires a lot of water and a tropical climate. In Africa, other cereals such as millet are more common. In colder parts of northern Europe, rye is grown and used to make rye bread.

POTATOES

The potato is a tuber formed by an underground stem. The plant uses the tuber as a store of starch. In summer, the potato plant grows rapidly and it forms many underground stems from which the tubers develop. As it makes sugars in photosynthesis, the food is moved underground and stored in the tubers. In autumn, the shoot dies back but the tubers survive the winter underground. In spring, the starch in the tubers is used to fuel the new growth of the plant. People grow potatoes because they are an excellent source of carbohydrate as well as being easy and cheap to grow.

GLASSHOUSES AND HYDROPONICS

Many crops, especially the more valuable salad crops, are grown in large glasshouses where the internal environment can be monitored and controlled. This includes the number of hours of light, the level of carbon dioxide in the air, and the temperature. Growing crops like this allows the crop to be grown out of season. For example, lettuces can be grown all year round under glass, whereas outside they are normally only grown in the summer.

Now it is even possible to grow plants without soil. These plants are grown in large containers filled with a water containing nutrients. Growing plants in this way is called hydroponics. The water circulates around the roots of the plants bringing the correct balance of nutrients and oxygen. By circulating the water, the nutrients are continually monitored and balanced.

FERTILIZERS, WEEDS, AND PESTS

Crop plants need to be given ideal growing conditions if they are to produce the biggest possible crop or maximum yield. They have to be grown in suitable soils and supplied with enough water and the correct nutrients.

HERBICIDES

It is also important to remove any other plants that could compete with the crop plants for nutrients, water, and space. These plants are called weeds. The easiest way to get rid of them is to kill them using weedkillers, or herbicides. There are many different types of herbicide. Some only kill specific types of weeds, while others kill all the plants with which they come into contact. These can cause problems because they may also kill the crop plants.

Pest control is not just for crops – these workers at Disneyland, Paris, are sprinkling mites onto decorative plants. The mites will eat the pests and protect the plants!

PEST CONTROL

Crops also need to be protected from pests such as insects, **fungi**, bacteria, and **viruses**. Pests can damage the crop and reduce the amount produced. The most common way to remove pests is to use an artificial pesticide made from poisonous chemicals. This will kill all the pest species, but often also kills a lot of other organisms. However, there is a more natural way to control pests. Using biological control is when the farmer introduces a natural predator of the pest to keep the numbers down. For example, the whitefly is a major pest of salad crops, such as tomatoes, grown in glasshouses. They can be controlled without the use of chemicals by the introduction of a small wasp called *Encarsia*, which feeds on the whitefly.

ENVIRONMENTALLY FRIENDLY

In recent years, modern farming has moved away from its reliance on fertilizers and pesticides that were used in great quantities during the 1950s and 1960s. People have recognized that the use of these chemicals has harmed the environment in many ways, for example by killing beneficial insects such as bees, poisoning seed-eating birds, and polluting streams and rivers. Now the trend is to use fewer chemicals and, if possible, none at all. One way forward is integrated pest management (IPM). This is where a farmer makes use of both pesticides and natural control methods. Only tiny amounts of pesticides are used. Farmers may not spray the edges of fields, which, in turn, allows natural predators of the crop pests to thrive. Farmers may also leave beetle banks, which are rough strips of grass left in the middle of large cereal fields where useful animals, such as ground beetles (predators of crop pests), can live.

Companion planting is when certain plants are used to keep away insect pests of other plants. This picture shows marigolds planted with onions in an organic garden. Marigolds are believed to repel a type of worm that attacks roots.

GOING ORGANIC

There has also been a rapid rise in the number of organic farms. These farms do not use any artificial fertilizers and rely on natural predators rather than pesticides to control pests. Organic farming does not produce such large yields but is far better for the environment. The variety of wildlife found on an organic farm is much greater than a farm using chemicals. Organic food is often not perfectly formed and may have blemishes, but it is free of chemicals so it is healthier and may taste better. By buying organic food, people are helping to support those farmers who care for their environment.

VEGETARIANS AND VEGANS

Nowadays, people are looking carefully at the food they eat and some are deciding not to eat animal products. These are people who have decided to eat vegetarian or vegan diets. Vegetarians are people who do not eat meat, poultry, or fish or their by-products. Some may not eat any animal products such as dairy foods or eggs. A vegan does not eat any animal flesh (meat, poultry, fish, and seafood) or products (eggs and dairy). Often they avoid honey and yeast products, as well as not wearing or using any animal products such as leather, silk, and wool.

Many people follow a vegetarian or vegan diet because it is healthy. It is typically low in saturated and total fat, high in dietary fibre and complex carbohydrate, and high in protective minerals and vitamins found in fresh fruit and vegetables. Some people may have environmental reasons. For example, the amounts of land, energy, and water used to raise farm animals is many times greater than that needed to raise crops.

GM CROPS

One of the more controversial issues in recent years has been genetically modified (GM) crops. These are plants that have been altered by **genetic engineering** so that they have new characteristics. GM crops are grown widely in North America, parts of South America, China, and India. However, they are still being studied in the European Union. There is some concern in Europe and the US about how they may affect the environment and whether they are safe to eat.

GM plants have had the **DNA** in their **genes** altered. For example, there is a GM maize that is resistant to a weedkiller containing glyphosate. Glyphosate is a weedkiller that will kill all plants it comes into contact with. It does not harm insects or other animals and it breaks down quickly. This means that it is less harmful to the environment than most weedkillers. But glyphosate cannot be sprayed on crops because it would kill the crop too, so farmers have to use other, more harmful, weedkillers. The GM maize with the new gene can be safely sprayed with glyphosate.

The gene that gives resistance to glyphosate was found in a bacterium. It was cut out of the bacterial DNA and inserted into the crop plant's DNA. This enabled the plant to produce a new protein that protects it from the effects of glyphosate. Genetic modification has enabled crops to be given new qualities that traditional breeding could not achieve in such a short period of time.

GM CROPS – PROS AND CONS

GM technology is still new and controversial, but it could benefit the environment. A pest-resistant cotton means that the farmer only has to use a little pesticide, while weedkiller-resistant crops allow farmers to use glyphosate, which breaks down quickly. However, there are fears that the pollen from these new crops could pollinate non-GM crops growing nearby. This would be a problem for an organic farmer who must not allow their crops to be contaminated in this way. It is also possible that weedkiller-resistant genes may create super weeds that cannot be killed by the usual weedkillers.

SCIENCE PIONEERS Paul Berg and the path to GM crops

The revolution in genetic engineering dates back to 1972, when biochemist Paul Berg at Stanford University in the United States discovered how to join together DNA from two different organisms. In 1983, a research team announced that they had created the first genetically modified plant – a tobacco plant resistant to the antibiotic kanamycin. The first field trial of a GM organism took place in 1986. It involved spraying strawberry plants with genetically modified bacteria to protect them from frost damage. In 1994, the first commercially available GM food appeared in the United States. It was the Flavr Savr tomato, genetically engineered to keep it firm for longer. Since that time many GM crops have been produced and they are now grown all around the world.

There are groups of people that protest against GM crops because they believe that the modified plants are not safe for the environment.

Wood, fuel, and medicines

Plants do not just provide food. They give us wood, fuel, cotton, linen, and other fibres. Plant products can be used to make fuel for cars and industry. Also they are an incredibly rich source of medicines – in fact, one third of all medicines were originally derived from plants.

WOOD

Wood is an incredibly versatile material. It has been used for thousands of years to build homes, boats, bridges, fencing, as well as furniture, musical instruments, and much more.

The wood of trees such as oak and beech is called hardwood because it is hard and heavy. The wood of the ironwood tree is so heavy that it sinks in water. Conifers, such as pine and spruce, produce a softer wood that does not last so long. However, conifers grow faster than hardwood species. Often conifer trees are harvested within 20 to 30 years of being planted, whereas hardwood trees are not ready for cutting until they are 50 or 60 years old. This means that softwood is much cheaper.

SUSTAINABLE GROWING

Many trees, such as conifers and eucalyptus, are grown in large plantations where the trees are planted and harvested together. The whole area can then be replanted. This is a sustainable method of growing trees, as the trees are replanted and can be harvested again. The harvesting of tropical hardwood trees found in rainforests is not usually sustainable as the trees are not normally replaced and the land is put to other uses.

WOOD AS FUEL

About 40 percent of the world's people rely on wood as their main source of fuel for heating and cooking. This wood is usually gathered every day from the neighbouring area.

In areas of high population the lack of wood means that some people have to walk many kilometres each day to find enough wood with which to cook and heat water. This leads to massive **deforestation** and causes endless environmental problems.

Fuel wood is running out as the human population increases and more wood is cut each day.

FOSSIL FUELS

Coal is a fossil fuel that is derived from plants. Millions of years ago in swampy areas, trees died and became buried in mud. The wood was slowly squashed as more mud built up. In time this led to the formation of peat and then coal. Today, coal is an important fuel and is used to fuel power stations that generate electricity. It is believed that the coal reserves will last about 250 years. However, this is an unsustainable source of fuel, as the coal reserves cannot be replaced. One day in the future, coal supplies will run out.

FUEL AND OIL

Many plant seeds are rich in oils that can be extracted and used in many ways. For example, for hundreds of years the oil taken from the seeds of rapeseed was burnt in lamps and used as a cooking oil. Today, rapeseed is the third largest source of vegetable oil in the world, and is used to make margarine, lubricants, and livestock food. More recently, it has been used to make biodiesel fuel, which can be used as an alternative to petrol to power engines. This is a sustainable source of fuel as new crops can be grown each year. In Brazil, sugar from sugar cane is made into ethanol, an alcohol. This is mixed with petrol to make a fuel called gasohol. By using sugar cane to make fuel, Brazil can reduce the amount of oil that is imported into the country.

Biodiesel can be used on its own or blended with regular diesel fuel. Biofuels are safer for the environment than fossil fuels, but they are more expensive to produce.

DIESEL

BIO-DIESEL

...iesel-
...aftstoff

DIN
N 590

Dieser Kraftstoff entspricht

BIODIESEL

E DIN
51606

DESIGNER PLANTS

Some crop plants are being genetically modified to make products that are useful to industry. Oil seed rape is a crop that makes oil-rich seeds. Research is underway to insert new genes into this plant to enable it to make oils and other substances that have specific industrial uses. This involves finding the gene in another organism, such as a bacterium, fungus, or even another plant, removing it and then inserting it into the DNA of the crop plant. For example, the plant coriander produces a substance called petroselinic acid, which is used in the making of detergents, nylon, and other plastics. Coriander is not an easy plant to grow in large quantities but scientists are hoping to be able to insert the coriander gene into oil seed rape, which can be grown on a large scale.

PLANT FIBRES

Plants can be used to make paper, rope, and textiles. Have a look at a tough leaf. If you turn it over, you can see veins running across the leaf. If you are careful, you can pull out the vein as a fibre. Some plants are more fibrous than others and are a useful source of fibres.

Paper is made from wood. The trees are cut and the trunk chopped into tiny pieces and then pulped to release the fibres. Then the fibres are bleached to make them white, mixed with water and squeezed flat. Cotton is made from the white fibres that form around the seed called the boll. Similarly, coconut mats are made from the fibres that form the shell of the coconut fruit. Soft fibres such as jute, linen, and hemp come from inside the stem of the plant. Tough sisal fibres, used to make mats and ropes, come from the long narrow leaves of agave plants.

Did you know..?

More than 5 new trees are planted each year for every man, woman, and child in the United States, and millions more regrow naturally from seeds and sprouts.

MEDICINAL PLANTS

Plants have been used for thousands of years to treat diseases and reduce pain. For example, the bark of the willow is a source of natural aspirin, while foxgloves are a source of digitalis, a medicine used to treat heart disease. Morphine comes from the opium poppy, while the bark of the cinchona tree was used to make quinine, the drug used to treat **malaria**.

TRADITIONAL AND MODERN MEDICINES

In the past, herb gardens were a common sight in towns and villages and they supplied the local people with a wide range of medicines. Today, people living in many parts of the world rely on plants as a free source of natural medicines.

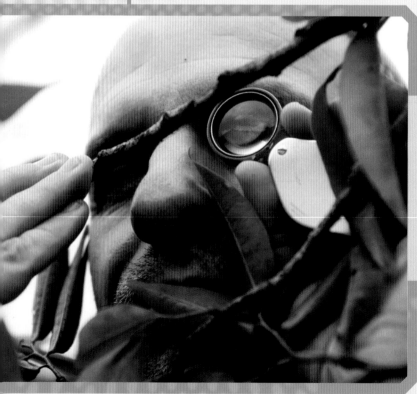

Rainforests around the world are being cut down at an alarming rate. There are many types of plants and trees in the rainforest, so scientists are searching to try to find new useful plants before they are lost forever.

About 13 percent of the flowering plants around the world are used medically – that is more than 53,000 different species – and most are used in traditional medicines. At least one-third, if not more, of all the medicines sold around the world were first derived from plants.

Drug companies are constantly screening thousands of species of plants, looking for products that might have medical uses. They send scientists to the rainforests and remote places to look for useful plants, which are then taken back to the laboratory and investigated further. The scientists talk to local people to find out which plants they use. One of the richest sources is the world's rainforests. There is a huge variety of plants growing in these habitats and many could have medicinal uses. This untapped source of new drugs is just one reason why it is important for the rainforests to be preserved.

FROM PLANT TO PRESCRIPTION

The discovery of a plant with potential to become a medicine is just the start of a very long process. The medicinal substance in the plant has to be extracted and tested to see if it is safe to use on people. This testing can take many years before the new product is ready to be used and prescribed by doctors. Often, it is not possible to collect the plant from the wild. This means the drug companies have to find ways of growing the plant commercially under controlled conditions so that they can produce an all-year-round supply of the medicine.

Tomorrow's plants

Over the next few years, it is likely that a greater range of GM crops will be produced for food and other uses. Many of the new plants may be designed to improve human health. For example, many millions of people eat a diet that is lacking in vitamin A and this deficiency causes blindness. This problem could be eliminated by the creation of a new variety of GM rice, called golden rice, which is high in vitamin A.

GM crops cost a lot to produce so the seed is expensive and poor farmers cannot afford them. Many of the crops that are grown in African countries, such as sorghum, millet, and cassava, have not been improved, unlike the wheat and rice crops. The farmers cannot afford to use fertilizers and pesticides, so the yield of these crops is much lower than it could be. Developing a GM millet or cassava plant could improve yields in some of the world's poorest countries and help to reduce poverty and starvation.

Some plants may be modified to make substances that are difficult to produce in a factory. Others may be used to replace products that are usually derived from fossil fuels such as oil and gas. More land may be given over to growing energy crops that are used to generate electricity. These crops are a sustainable source of fuel as they can be regrown.

Did you know..?

The total area of GM crops grown around the world has increased from 1.7 million hectares (4.2 million acres) in 1996 to 81 million hectares (200 million acres) in 2004. The United States grows nearly 60 percent of the world's GM crops.

VACCINES IN A BANANA

Imagine going to the doctors to have a **vaccination** and instead of the **vaccine** being injected into your arm, you are asked to eat a banana! This may not be as far-fetched as it sounds. Bananas are being genetically modified to produce a vaccine in their fruit. This has many advantages. Bananas can be grown in large numbers and the fruits can be transported easily. The vaccine does not need to be stored in a refrigerator, nor are there problems about using sterile needles. The banana plants can also be grown in some of the poorest countries where the people cannot afford vaccines.

Local banana growers in poorer countries may be able to help provide vaccines to prevent various diseases and save lives.

PLANTS FOR THE FUTURE

Plants are essential to our everyday lives. We rely on plants to provide us with much of our food, building materials, and clothing. They may be essential to our survival in the future. By planting more forests we may be able to take up more carbon dioxide from the atmosphere and reduce the effects of global warming. Once our supplies of oil and gas run out, we may rely on plant oils to fuel our cars and homes.

Further resources

MORE BOOKS TO READ

Harper, Janet, *Interdependence* (Letts Educational, 2005)

Spilsbury, Louise and Richard, *The Life of Plants* series (Heinemann Library, 2003)

Stockley, Corinne, *The Usborne Illustrated Dictionary of Biology* (Usborne Publishing, 2005)

Nature Encyclopedia (Dorling Kindersley, 1998)

USING THE INTERNET

Explore the Internet to find out more about green plants.
You can use a search engine, such as www.yahooligans.com or www.google.com, and type in keywords such as *photosynthesis*, *chlorophyll*, *transpiration*, *pollination*, or *GM crops*.

These search tips will help you find useful websites more quickly:

- Know exactly what you want to find out about first.
- Use only a few important keywords in a search, putting the most relevant words first.
- Be precise. Only use names of people, places, or things.

Disclaimer
All the internet addresses (URLs) given in this book were valid at the time of going to press. However, due to the dynamic nature of the Internet, some addresses may have changed, or sites may have ceased to exist since publication. While the author and publishers regret any inconvenience this may cause readers, no responsibility for any such changes can be accepted by either the author or the publishers.

Glossary

adapt   change to suit a particular habitat or environment

amino acid   building block of proteins

bacteria   type of micro-organism that can be helpful, but that can also cause disease

biomass   total mass of living organisms in an area

botanist   scientist who studies plants

carbohydrate   chemical, such as sugar or starch, which contains carbon, hydrogen, and oxygen

carpel   female part of a flower consisting of a stigma, style, and ovary. The ovule is located inside the ovary.

cellulose   substance found in the cell walls of plants, made of lots of units of sugars joined together in chains

chlorophyll   chemical used by plants to capture the Sun's energy

chloroplast   structure in the plant cell that contains chlorophyll

climate   what the weather is like in a particular place over a length of time

cytoplasm   jelly-like substance which fills the cell and in which the components of the cell are suspended

deforestation   destruction of forests

dehydrated   lacking in water

dicotyledon   plant that has two embryo leaves inside its seeds

DNA (deoxyribonucleic acid)   molecule that carries the genetic code. It is found in the nucleus of the cell.

dormant   in a deep sleep

drought   when there is no rain for an extended period of time

embryo   fertilized egg in its early stages of development

enzyme   protein molecule that changes the rate of chemical reactions in living things without being affected itself in the process

evolve   change over time

fertilization   joining together of a male and female sex cell

fertilizer   chemicals or natural substances, such as manure, which are rich in nutrients and are added to the soil to improve plant growth

food chain   links between different animals that feed on each other and on plants

fossil fuels   fuels formed over millions of years from the remains of ancient plants and animals. They are oil, coal, and natural gas.

fruit   structure formed from the ovary of a flower following fertilization which protects the seed

fungi   type of organisms that are not plants or animals – they do not move around and cannot photosynthesise

gene   individual unit of inheritance

genetic engineering   technique for changing the genetic information in a cell

germinate   when a seed starts to grow

inorganic   not from natural growth

kingdom   name given to the five main groups of living organisms – the biggest groups in classification

malaria   fever caused by a protozoan parasite, more common in warmer countries

micro-organism   bacteria, viruses, and other minute organisms which can be seen only using a microscope

mineral   inorganic substance required by living organisms for healthy life and growth

molecule   group of atoms bonded together

monocotyledon   plant that has a single tiny leaf inside their seeds

nucleus   central part of the cell which contains the DNA

nutrient   substance that provides an organism with the nourishment essential for life and growth

ovary   part of the female reproductive system that produces ovules

ovule   female sex cell

parasite   organism which lives in or on another organism

parasitic   organism which acts as a parasite

permeable   allowing the passage of something (for example water or gases)

phloem   type of tube that carries sugar around the plant

photosynthesis   process by which green plants make food from carbon dioxide and water, using energy from the Sun

pollination   the transfer of pollen from the anthers of one flower to the stigma of another

producer   first organism in the food chain. Plants are producers as they harness energy from the Sun to make food.

protein   a large molecule made from chains of amino acids

reproduction   producing new individuals

respiration   process involved in the production of energy in living things. Oxygen is taken in and carbon dioxide given off.

savannah   grassy plain with few trees

seed   structure that contains the embryo of a plant, formed from the ovule of a flower

soluble   can dissolve in a particular substance, for example water

species   specific group of very closely related organisms whose members can breed successfully to produce fertile offspring

spore   tiny reproductive unit, typically just one cell

stamen   the male part of a flower, consisting of an anther and a filament

starch   carbohydrate made by plants, made up of many glucose molecules joined together in a chain

temperate   region with mild temperatures, neither very hot nor cold

transpiration   evaporation of water from the surfaces of a plant

tuber   undergound stem of a plant

tundra   treeless Arctic region of Europe, Asia, and North America

turgid   swollen, for example a cell full of water

ultraviolet   rays that are beyond the visible light spectrum

vaccination   to inject a vaccine

vaccine   substance that usually contains weakened or dead bacteria or viruses that is injected into the body to prevent a disease

vacuole   large fluid-filled space, surrounded by a membrane found in plant cells

vascular bundle   group of tissues including phloem, xylem, and packing tissue, that form veins in leaves

virus   tiny particle usually made up of DNA or RNA coated in protein. Viruses multiply by infecting other cells.

xylem   vessels the cells, strengthened with lignin that transport water and minerals around a plant, found in a vascular bundle

Index

Titles in the *Life Science in Depth* series include:

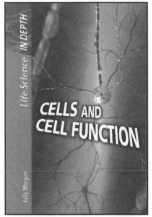

Hardback   0 431 10896 X

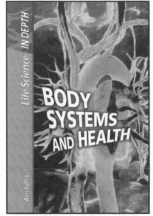

Hardback   0 431 10897 8

Hardback   0 431 10898 6

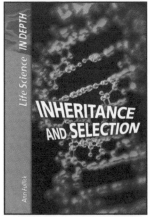

Hardback   0 431 10899 4

Hardback   0 431 10900 1

Hardback   0 431 10901 X

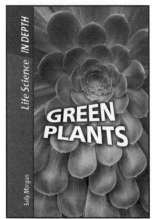

Hardback   0 431 10910 9

Find out about other titles from Heinemann Library on our website www.heinemann.co.uk/library